Water Worlds
Mangroves

Beth Blaxland
for the Australian Museum

This edition first published in 2002 in the United States of America by Chelsea House Publishers, a subsidiary of Haights Cross Communications

Reprinted 2003

Chelsea House Publishers
1974 Sproul Road, Suite 400
Broomall, PA 19008–0914

The Chelsea House world wide web address is www.chelseahouse.com

Library of Congress Cataloging-in-Publication Data Applied for.
ISBN 0-7910-6565-0

First published in 2000 by
Macmillan Education Australia Pty Ltd
627 Chapel Street, South Yarra, Australia, 3141

Copyright © Australian Museum 2000

Australian Museum Series Editor: Carolyn MacLulich
Australian Museum Scientific Adviser: Doug Hoese
Australian Museum Publishing Unit: Jenny Saunders and Kate Lowe

Edited by Anne McKenna
Typeset in Bembo
Printed in Hong Kong
Text and cover design by Leigh Ashforth @ watershed art & design
Illustrations by Peter Mather

Acknowledgements

The author and publishers are grateful to the following for permission to use copyright material:
Front cover:
      Main photo: Jiri Lochman/Lochman Transparencies
      Inset photo: John Shaw/AUSCAPE
Back cover: Clay Bryce/Lochman Transparencies

Kathie Atkinson, pp. 6, 10, 11 (bottom), 15, 17 (left), 21; Hans & Judy Beste/Lochman Transparencies, p. 22 (bottom); Roger Brown/AUSCAPE, p. 20 (right); Clay Bryce/Lochman Transparencies, p. 16; Densey Clyne/AUSCAPE, pp. 11 (top), 12; Ben Cropp/AUSCAPE, pp. 19 (left), 27; Ben & Lynn Cropp/AUSCAPE, pp. 3, 26; Jean-Paul Ferrero/AUSCAPE, pp. 7 (bottom), 19 (right), 23; Ferrero-Labat/AUSCAPE, p. 8; Greg Harold/AUSCAPE, p. 25 (top); C. Andrew Henley/AUSCAPE, p. 22 (top); Mike Langford/AUSCAPE, pp. 4, 5; Jiri Lochman/Lochman Transparencies, pp. 7 (top), 13 (bottom), 24; Marie Lochman/Lochman Transparencies, p. 30; D. Parer & E. Parer-Cook/AUSCAPE, pp. 14, 25 (bottom); Jamie Plaza van Roon/AUSCAPE, p. 13 (top); Dennis Sarson/Lochman Transparencies, p. 18; John Shaw/AUSCAPE, p. 20 (left).

Contents

What are mangroves?

There are many different types of plants called **mangroves**. Some are tall trees that grow 30 meters (98 feet) high; others are small shrubs only one meter (3 feet) high. Some have bright green leaves; others have leaves that are dark green on top and silver underneath. Some mangroves even have roots that grow up out of the ground instead of down into the ground.

These different types of plants are all mangroves because they live on the land but are flooded by sea water for part of each day. Sea water floods the mangroves every time the tide comes in. Then, as the tide goes out, the sea water drains away and the land appears again. The land that mangroves live on is called the shore.

≋ It is high tide and these mangrove trees are flooded by sea water. The water is brown because there is mud mixed in with the sea water.

These are young mangrove seedlings. Their leaves are only just above the water.

Mangroves are different to other plants because they live on land for part of the day and in sea water for part of the day. Mangroves are **adapted** to living in these places. This means that they are used to this special type of **habitat** and are able to live, grow and reproduce there.

Did you know?

The land at the edge of the sea is called the shore. The water on the shore gets higher when the tide comes in. This is called high tide. The water on the shore gets lower when the tide goes out. This is called low tide.

*A high tide is always followed by a low tide and a low tide is always followed by another high tide. In most places there are two high tides and two low tides each day. The part of the shore that lies between high tide and low tide is called the **intertidal** (say: in-ter-ty-dal) **zone**.*

≋ It is now low tide and the ground can now be seen under these mangrove trees. The ground is very muddy.

These are mangrove tree roots sticking up out of the mud. They are unusual because they grow up into the air instead of down into the ground.

Where mangroves grow

Mangroves grow in places with the following conditions:

- soft ground
- shelter from strong waves
- shallow shores in the intertidal zone
- warm temperatures all year round.

Soft ground

Mangroves need soft ground for their roots to grow in. Some mangroves grow in sand but most grow in mud.

Muddy soils are often found along the banks of an **estuary** (say: est-shu-ree). An estuary is the place where fresh water from a river mixes with salty water from the sea.

An estuary usually has muddy soil along its banks because streams and rivers carry tiny bits of soil called **sediment**. This sediment gets into the rivers when dust is blown in or soil is washed in. The sediment is then carried all the way down to the estuary. Some of it is washed out to sea but the rest builds up along the edges of the estuary.

Did you know?

Sometimes a mangrove tree seems to grow on hard rock or coral, but if you look closely, its roots are really growing in tiny cracks filled with sandy or muddy soil.

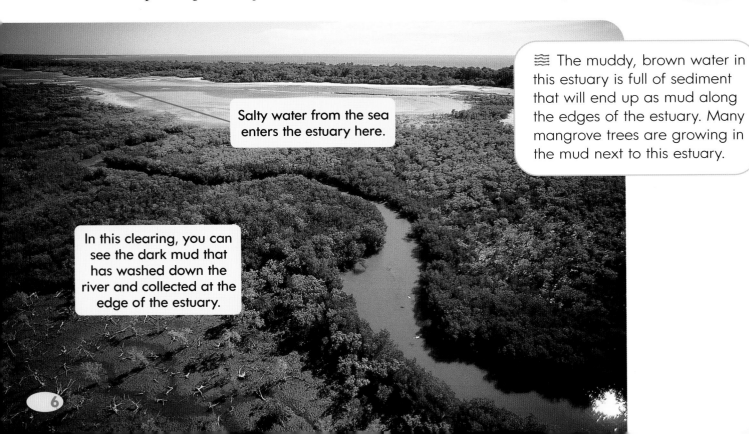

Salty water from the sea enters the estuary here.

≋ The muddy, brown water in this estuary is full of sediment that will end up as mud along the edges of the estuary. Many mangrove trees are growing in the mud next to this estuary.

In this clearing, you can see the dark mud that has washed down the river and collected at the edge of the estuary.

Shelter

Mangroves need sheltered places because strong waves can wash away the mud or sand that mangroves grow in. If the soft ground was washed away, the mangrove seedlings would fall over and be washed into the sea. If the waves were strong enough they could even break the branches of big mangrove trees or push the trees over.

Places that are sheltered from strong waves include estuaries and bays. Sheltered places are also found where big islands or coral reefs form a barrier that stops strong ocean waves getting through to the shore.

≋ The trees growing at the bottom of this giant sand dune are mangroves. They are growing in a sheltered bay that is protected from waves.

The plants on the sand dune are growing up above the high tide level. They are not mangroves.

≋ This estuary is also sheltered from the sea's waves. Lots of mangrove trees are growing along the edges of this estuary.

Shallow shores

Mangroves grow in the intertidal zone. The intertidal zone is the part of the shore that is covered by sea water at high tide and uncovered at low tide.

Mangroves grow best on shallow shores in the intertidal zone. A shallow shore is a shore where the water does not get very deep at high tide.

Shallow shores are often very flat. Flat shores have a wide intertidal zone with plenty of room for many mangrove trees to grow. On steep shores, the intertidal zone is very narrow. This means there is not much room for mangrove trees to grow.

≋ This shallow shore is very flat and lots of bright green mangrove trees are growing here.

The steep hill behind these mangroves is covered by rainforest. The hill is above the high tide level so it does not have any mangroves on it.

Warm temperatures

Mangroves grow best in warm places like the **tropics**. Places further away from the tropics can get very cold in winter. If winter temperatures get colder than 16 degrees Celsius (60°F), most mangroves cannot grow.

In Australia, most mangroves grow in the tropics, north of the Tropic of Capricorn. There are more than 30 different types of mangrove trees and shrubs growing in Australia's tropics.

Further away from the tropics, there are fewer and fewer different types of mangroves. For example, in southern New South Wales, only two types of mangroves grow. Even further south in Victoria, South Australia and the southern parts of Western Australia, only one type of mangrove can grow in the colder temperatures. In Tasmania, the air and water temperatures are too cold and no mangroves can grow.

≋ These mangroves are growing in the tropics at Cape Tribulation in northern Queensland, Australia. The temperature here is warm all year round and helps the mangroves grow into tall trees. In southern Australia, mangroves only grow into small shrubs because the winters are cold.

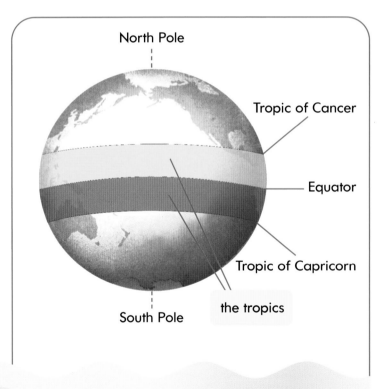

North Pole

Tropic of Cancer

Equator

Tropic of Capricorn

the tropics

South Pole

Did you know?

The tropics are found in the middle part of the Earth between the Tropic of Cancer and the Tropic of Capricorn. The tropics get more sun than the other parts of the Earth. This means that places in the tropics are warm or hot the whole year round.

How mangroves are adapted to their habitat

The leaves, roots and seeds of mangrove plants are adapted to their habitat. This means they have special ways of helping mangroves live where they do.

≋ When this Grey Mangrove takes in too much salt from the soil, it moves the salt to its leaves. These leaves store the salt. When they have too much salt in them, the leaves turn yellow and fall off the tree. This gets the salt out of the tree so it will not die. Can you see the bright yellow leaves on this tree?

Mangrove leaves

The soil that mangroves grow in is very salty from the sea water that covers it each day. Most land plants cannot live in ground with salty soil.

The leaves of mangroves are adapted to living in a salty habitat. There are two ways that mangrove leaves help mangrove plants to live where they do:

- some store salt
- some **excrete** or remove salt.

≋ The leaves of Grey Mangroves also excrete salt. You can see the salt on these leaves.

≋ Salty water gets pushed out of tiny holes in the leaf. The water then evaporates or dries up and the salt is left behind on the surface of the leaf. This salt then gets washed off the leaf when it rains.

Did you know?

Salty soils make land plants dry out. Land animals that eat or drink a lot of salt also dry out. This includes people. Think about how thirsty you get when you eat a lot of very salty food.

Too much salt can even kill plants and animals. Plants can easily be killed with salt. Some people pour salt water on weeds growing in their gardens to kill them, but they have to be careful not to kill their favorite garden plants.

Mangrove roots

The soil that mangroves grow in is salty, soft and wet. Most other plants would die in this type of soil. This is because the salt would kill them, they would fall over in the soft ground and they could not grow in ground that is always wet.

Mangroves have roots that are adapted to salty, soft and wet ground. There are two ways that mangrove roots help mangrove trees to grow where they do:

- The underground roots of some mangroves can filter out salt.
- Many mangroves also have special above-ground roots. These help hold the plant in the ground and also get oxygen from the air.

Some different types of above-ground roots are: knee roots, stilt roots and peg roots. Peg roots are also called **pneumatophores** (say: nyoo-ma-to-forz).

The tangle of mangrove roots traps sediment carried down by rivers or brought in at high tide. This way, mangroves can add to the land area and also help protect the shore from washing away.

Did you know?

Ground that is always wet does not have much oxygen in it. Oxygen is needed by the roots of land plants to help them grow. If the roots cannot get enough oxygen, the whole plant dies.

≋ These are Large-leaved Mangroves. Their underground roots filter out salt. This keeps the salt from getting into the mangrove plant when its roots take in water.

Large-leaved Mangroves have knee roots as well as underground roots. These above-ground roots grow up in the air, bend like a knee and grow down again.

Stilt roots grow down from the trunk and branches then into the ground. They often loop across the ground.

≋ These Red Mangroves have stilt roots that get oxygen from the air and underground roots that filter out salt.

Grey Mangroves have lots of peg roots or pneumatophores. They look like little sticks growing up out of the ground. High tide covers the pneumatophores but at low tide they can get oxygen from the air.

≋ Grey Mangroves filter out salt using their underground roots.

Did you know?

If their above-ground roots are flooded by water for too long or buried under sediment, the mangroves cannot get enough oxygen and they die. Mangroves can also die if there is oil pollution in the water. The oil sticks to their above-ground roots and stops them getting oxygen.

Mangrove seeds

A plant that is adapted to its habitat must be able to reproduce. Mangrove trees reproduce by making seeds that grow into new mangrove trees.

Mangrove seeds are adapted to living in a habitat where the tide always comes in and out.

The seeds of this mangrove have started growing while still on the tree. This is a Red Mangrove and its seedlings can grow up to 30 centimeters (one foot) long before they drop into the water.

The seedlings float until they are washed up on the shore. Then the large seedlings quickly grow roots that stop them from getting washed away by the tides.

There are two ways that mangrove seeds are adapted to their habitat:

- The seeds of some kinds of mangroves start growing while they are still on the parent mangrove tree.
- Mangrove seeds and seedlings can float in water.

Did you know?

Some Aboriginal peoples from the northern parts of Australia use the seeds of Grey Mangroves and Large-leaved Mangroves as food. These mangrove seeds are collected from the seashore, cooked and then eaten.

The seeds on this Grey Mangrove grow to about three centimeters (one inch) long. The seeds start to grow into seedlings while they are still on the tree.

When a seedling falls off the tree, it can float in the sea water for about three days. This gives it a chance to land somewhere where it can grow.

If there is a lot of shade, the seedlings only grow to about 30 or 40 centimeters (12 to 15 inches) high. They stay small until the tree above them dies and more light can get down to them. When this happens, they quickly grow up.

Neighboring habitats

Mangrove habitats are found between two other habitats: seagrass meadows and saltmarshes. Many of the animals living in mangrove habitats visit these neighboring habitats.

Seagrass meadows are found in the intertidal zone and in the sea. Saltmarshes are found on the land side of mangroves and sometimes get flooded by very high tides.

≋ This diagram shows the different habitats near mangroves.

high tide ———

low tide ———

woodland

saltmarsh

mangroves

seagrass meadow

Did you know?

Seagrass meadows are called nursery areas. This is because many young fishes and prawns live in the seagrass meadows while they are growing bigger.

Seagrass meadows

The plants that grow in seagrass meadows are called seagrasses. These plants look like grasses but live in the sea. They grow in soft mud or sand and are found in sheltered areas with shallow water. Sometimes lots of seagrass leaves get washed up onto the shore.

Saltmarshes

Saltmarsh habitats are found on land but they look very different to mangrove habitats. There are no trees in saltmarsh habitats because it is too far from the shore for mangrove trees to grow and the ground is too salty for other trees to grow. The plants that grow in saltmarsh habitats are small, growing only half a meter (1.6 feet) or less.

≋ This is a kind of seagrass called Strap Weed. It grows below the level of low tide. This means it is always covered by sea water.

This is Seablite. It is a saltmarsh plant that stores the water it needs in its leaves.

This is Samphire (say: sam-fire). It is a saltmarsh plant that stores water in its thick stems. The plant needs this water so it will not dry out in its salty habitat.

Puddles of salty water are found on the lower parts of saltmarshes. Salt is left lying on top of the ground when the water in the puddle evaporates.

Life in a mangrove habitat

A mangrove habitat gets its name because the first living things you see there are mangrove plants. However, many other living things are also found in mangrove habitats.

These other living things can sometimes be hard to find unless you know where to look. To find them, you need to look in three places:

- on the mangrove plants
- on and under the ground
- in the water that floods the mangroves at high tide.

Some animals are found in more than one place in the mangrove habitat. For example, egrets are birds that can be found on the mangrove plants, on the ground or wading in the shallow water under the mangroves. They are water birds that have long legs to wade in the water while they look for food. They eat fish and other small animals that they catch with their long pointed beaks.

≋ Egrets are often found on mangrove plants. They build their nests in them or use them for shelter when they need to rest.

Some animals live in mangrove habitats all the time. Others only stay for part of their lives to find food, shelter or somewhere to reproduce.

For example, when they are young, Mud Crabs live in mangrove habitats. They shelter in burrows they make in the soft ground and look for food at low tide. They eat small animals such as sea snails and small crabs.

Older Mud Crabs grow into big crabs with a body that is 20 centimeters (7.8 inches) wide. These big crabs do not need to shelter and feed near the mangroves. Instead they spend more time in the deeper water away from the mangrove habitat.

≋ Some animals are found in the water that floods the mangroves at high tide. They swim in looking for food and shelter.

≋ This Mud Crab only has one of its large front claws. It might have lost its other claw in a fight with a bigger animal that wanted to eat it.

This Epaulette Shark is a type of fish. It has come in looking for small fish or other small animals that might be hiding in the mangrove roots.

Life on mangrove plants

Living things can be found on the flowers, leaves, branches, trunks and above-ground roots of mangrove plants. Birds are the most obvious animals found on mangrove plants. Other large animals found there include fruit bats that feed on mangrove fruit, and goannas that climb the trees looking for birds or insects to eat.

Hundreds of different kinds of birds can be found in mangrove habitats. Many of these visit the mangroves for a short time then fly off to a different habitat. Some live in mangrove habitats all their lives and never go anywhere else.

Some birds feed on the flowers or seeds of mangrove trees. Others are meat-eaters and may leave the trees to find fishes, prawns or insects to eat.

≋ Birds such as this Nankeen Night Heron visit mangrove habitats but also live in other habitats.

During the day, Nankeen Night Herons rest in leafy trees close to the water. At night, they hunt for food such as fishes.

≋ Australian Collared Kingfishers only live in mangrove habitats. They often rest on bare branch tops.

This one has caught a soldier crab to eat. It also eats other animals such as small fishes and insects.

Small **invertebrate** (say: in-ver-ter-brait) animals are also found in mangrove habitats. Invertebrate animals do not have a backbone. Some of the invertebrate animals found on mangrove flowers, leaves or branches are ants, beetles, bees, butterflies and spiders.

Invertebrate animals found on pneumatophores and other above-ground roots include oysters, barnacles and snails. Oysters and barnacles are **filter feeders**. This means they feed by sifting out tiny pieces of food from water. They can only feed when they are covered by water. Snails can be found on mangrove tree trunks, pneumatophores or leaves. These snails are mostly plant-eaters.

≋ These snails are feeding on the **algae** (say: al-gee) growing on this pneumatophore. Algae are plants that live in wet conditions and do not have leaves, stems or roots like most plants. Seaweeds are algae.

Life on and under the ground

Many living things can be found on or under the ground in mangrove habitats. They include mammals, birds, fishes and invertebrate animals that move over the ground at low tide looking for food. Small seaweeds also grow on the ground in mangrove habitats.

≋ False Water-Rats are rare Australian mammals that live in mangrove habitats and some other wet habitats near the sea. They rest during the day in a nest made of leaves and mud. At night they run around on the mud looking for food. They catch crabs at low tide and eat them.

≋ This sandpiper belongs to a group of birds called waders. Many waders walk about on the ground searching for food in mangrove habitats.

This sandpiper eats invertebrate animals living in the mud. It sticks its long beak into the mud to find them.

One of the strangest animals found in mangrove habitats is the mudskipper. Mudskippers live in mangrove habitats in the tropics. They are small fishes that swim in water just like other fish, but they also come out of the water and live on the ground.

On land, mudskippers move by skipping and jumping across the mud. They can also crawl over the mud by using their fins like crutches.

Mudskippers have eyes that stick out above their heads. This helps them to see further and to find snails and small crabs to eat.

Some mudskippers, like this one, can climb up mangrove pneumatophores. They do this by holding onto the pneumatophore with their fins. Getting higher above the ground helps them look for food.

Did you know?

Each year about two million waders migrate between Australia and countries in Europe or Asia where they breed. When winter comes, they fly thousands of miles south to Australia. They live in Australia for seven to nine months each year, then fly back.

Invertebrates

Many different kinds of crabs and snails can be found on top of the ground at low tide. A lot of these invertebrate animals eat **detritus** (say: de-tri-tus). Detritus is food made up of plants and animals that are rotting away.

A lot of detritus is made in mangrove habitats. Most of it comes from old mangrove leaves that fall off the trees onto the ground. When the leaves rot, they break up into little pieces and then into even smaller pieces that get mixed in with the sediment.

≋ Mud whelks eat detritus and algae. Mud whelks are snails that have long pointed shells. Hundreds of mud whelks can often be seen on the ground in mangrove habitats.

Look closely on the mud between these mangrove seedlings and pneumatophores. Can you see the mud whelks and their trails?

Did you know?

The wet ground in mangrove habitats can be very smelly. Mangrove habitats with muddy ground smell the most. This smell is caused by very tiny living things called bacteria. They live in the mud and cause the smell by making the detritus rot. If you walk on the mud, your feet will sink into the soft ground and let more of the smell out.

A lot of invertebrate animals live under the ground in mangrove habitats. Some of these animals are worms, shrimps and crabs. Many different kinds of crabs come out of their burrows to feed on top of the ground at low tide.

≋ Fiddler crabs are small crabs that live in burrows. At low tide, they come out of their burrows and eat algae and detritus from the ground.

Male fiddler crabs have one very large claw. They wave it to send messages to other fiddler crabs.

Their eyes stick up on the end of long stalks.

≋ At low tide, soldier crabs move about in large groups on top of the ground. These small crabs eat detritus that is mixed in with the sediment.

They use their claws to scoop up detritus and sediment into their mouths. They sort out the food from the sediment and then they spit this sediment out onto the ground. The sediment they spit out looks like tiny balls made of mud or sand.

Life in the water

Many living things come into mangrove habitats when the sea water floods the ground at high tide. They include many different kinds of fishes and invertebrate animals such as prawns, sea urchins and jellyfish. Most come in looking for food and shelter.

For example, sea urchins are invertebrate animals that sometimes visit mangrove habitats at high tide. They eat algae that grows on the roots of mangrove trees. They have sharp teeth to scrape the algae into their mouths.

≋ These spiky animals are called sea urchins. They have long, sharp spines to protect themselves. They also use their spines like legs to help them move about.

Mangrove habitats and nearby seagrass meadows are nursery areas for many different kinds of young fishes. The young fishes eat detritus or small animals. They come into mangrove habitats because there is plenty of food there. After they have grown, some of these fishes swim away to live in other habitats. Others stay nearby and swim into the mangrove habitat with every high tide.

≋ Mangrove Jacks are big fish found in mangrove habitats in the tropics. They swim in at high tide and look for food such as small fishes.

Did you know?

A lot of people like to eat fishes and prawns. Many fishes and prawns live in mangrove habitats for part of their lives.

Some of these fishes are Mangrove Jacks, Barramundi (say: ba-ra-mun-dee), bream (say: brim), snapper, flathead and mullet. The prawns that live part of their lives in mangrove habitats include tiger prawns, king prawns and school prawns.

Food web of mangrove habitats

A food web shows what the different living things in a habitat eat. Plants are always at the beginning of a food web. The plants in a mangrove habitat include mangrove trees and algae.

Many of the animals in the habitat eat plants. Different parts of the plants can be used as food. For example, some animals eat leaves and some eat wood. Others eat flowers, seeds or fruit. Living things that eat plants are called **herbivores** (say: her-bi-vorz).

Some living things eat animals. Often a big animal eats a small one. Living things that eat animals are called **carnivores** (say: kar-ni-vorz).

Many of the living things in mangrove habitats eat detritus. These living things are called **detrivores** (say: de-tri-vorz).

Plants and detritus

mangrove trees

detritus from mangrove trees

algae

≋ This food web only shows some of the plants and animals that live in mangrove habitats. Where would you add in other living things such as False Water-Rats, sea urchins or fruit bats?

Did you know?

In a food web, arrows point from the food to the living thing that eats it.

For example:

prawns ————————➤ birds

This means that prawns are eaten by birds, or prawns are food for birds.

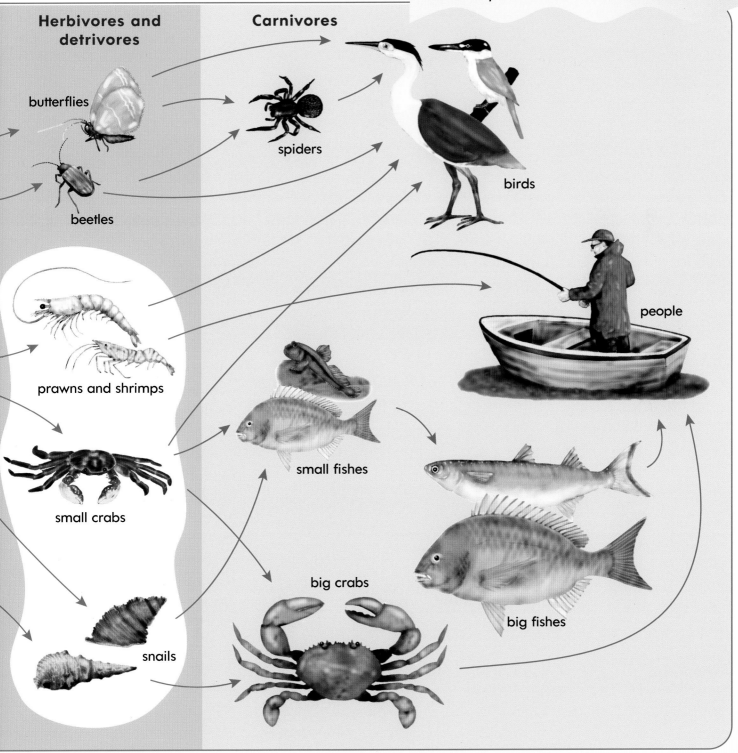

Herbivores and detrivores

butterflies

beetles

prawns and shrimps

small crabs

snails

Carnivores

spiders

birds

people

small fishes

big crabs

big fishes

Environment watch

Why are mangrove habitats important?

Mangrove habitats are important because:

- The mangrove roots hold the soft ground together and stop it from washing away into the sea.
- The above-ground roots of mangrove plants trap sediment from the rivers and the sea. This keeps the water in the estuaries and sea cleaner and makes it easier for plants and animals to live in mangrove habitats and neighboring habitats.
- They provide shelter for living things. For example, plants such as algae and mangrove trees find sheltered ground to grow in. Animals find shelter on the mangrove plants, on or under the ground, or in the water at high tide.
- They are used by living things as a place to reproduce. For example, mangrove seeds fall from the trees and start growing. Fishes and prawns use the mangrove habitats as nursery areas and some birds build their nests there.
- Many living things use them as places to find food. People eat fishes, prawns and other sea animals that live in mangrove habitats.

Things You Can Do
to help protect mangrove habitats

- ◇ Walk on the boardwalk (if there is one). Boardwalks are special paths that protect the ground and the mangrove plants from being damaged.
- ◇ Do not let rubbish get washed down storm drains and into rivers. This polluted water often ends up in mangrove habitats and can harm the plants and animals living there.
- ◇ Do not pour oil down the sink or drain. It can get into rivers or the sea and end up in mangrove habitats. This polluted water can kill the mangrove trees by covering their above-ground roots.
- ◇ Talk about mangrove habitats with your friends and family. Tell them why these habitats are important and how they can help protect them.

Glossary

adapted	when a living thing is used to a special habitat and can easily live there
algae	plants, such as seaweeds, that live in wet conditions and do not have leaves, stems or roots
carnivores	living things that eat animals
detritus	food made up of plants and animals that have rotted away into tiny pieces
detrivores	living things that eat detritus
estuary	the place where fresh water from a river mixes with salty water from the sea
excrete	force out waste matter
filter feeders	animals that eat by filtering out tiny pieces of food from the water around them
habitat	the place where a living thing lives, for example, a mangrove habitat
herbivores	living things that eat plants
intertidal zone	the area on the seashore or the bank of an estuary that is covered by water at high tide and uncovered at low tide
invertebrate	an animal that does not have a backbone, such as snails, crabs, prawns and worms
mangroves	trees or shrubs that are adapted to living in sheltered places with soft ground in the intertidal zone
pneumatophores	above-ground roots of some mangrove plants. They look like little sticks growing up out of the ground and are also called peg roots.
sediment	tiny bits of soil and rock
tropics	the area on the Earth between the Tropic of Cancer and the Tropic of Capricorn, where the temperatures are always warm or hot

Index